AMERICAN WOMEN OF THE GULF WAR

HEATHER HASAN

The Rosen Publishing Group, Inc., New York

*For Margorie and Richard James, with many thanks for all your support
and encouragement*

Published in 2004 by The Rosen Publishing Group, Inc.
29 East 21st Street, New York, NY 10010

Library of Congress Cataloging-in-Publication Data

Hasan, Heather.
American women of the Gulf War/Heather Hasan.—1st ed.
    p. cm.—(American women at war)
Summary: Profiles American women who served in the armed forces
during the Persian Gulf War, where more women were deployed to
combat and in more capacities than in any previous war. Includes
bibliographical references and index.
ISBN 0-8239-4447-6
1. Persian Gulf War, 1991—Women—Juvenile literature. 2. Women
soldiers—United States—Juvenile literature. [1. Persian Gulf War,
1991—Women. 2. Women and the military. 3. Women and war.
4. United States—Armed Forces—Women.]
I. Title. II. Series.
DS79.744.W65H37 2003
956.7044'22'0820973—dc22

                                                    2003015518

Manufactured in the United States of America

On the front cover: Staff Sergeant Fulce, 401st Airborne Squadron,
checks a 2,000-pound (907-kilogram) Mark 84 bomb.
On the back cover: A reproduction of an original Purple Heart medal.

Contents

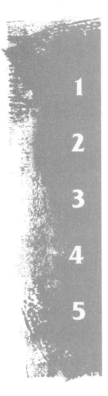

INTRODUCTION: THE ROLE OF WOMEN IN THE PERSIAN GULF WAR

Women had served in virtually every U.S. military operation since the Revolutionary War, but never before had they participated as much as they did in the Persian Gulf War. The Gulf War began on August 2, 1990, when Saddam Hussein, who became the president and dictator of Iraq in 1979, moved hundreds of Iraqi tanks into the neighboring country of Kuwait. Hussein hoped to make his country whole again by taking over Kuwait, a country he believed was part of Iraq. Though Kuwait was a wealthy country with many oil fields, it was

defenseless against Hussein's attack. In less than four hours, the Iraqi army had taken control of Kuwait's capital, Kuwait City, and its oil fields.

Hussein's actions were immediately condemned by the United States and its allies. Together, Iraq and Kuwait controlled more than 20 percent of the world's oil supply. If Saddam Hussein had continued his aggression into Saudi Arabia, as it seemed he might, he would have been in control of nearly half of the world's oil. If this oil were to have been taken off the world's market, the results could have been economically catastrophic.

In response to the invasion of Kuwait, a coalition against Iraq and Saddam Hussein was formed. Led by

In the Arab world, Iraqi president Saddam Hussein is viewed with mixed feelings. Some Middle Easterners praised Hussein for his commitment to unifying the Arab world and his refusal to buckle under Western influence. However, some members of the Arab world opposed Hussein's tyrannical rule and gross mistreatment of minority groups within Iraq.

U.S. president George H. W. Bush, the coalition consisted of thirty-two nations, including the United States, Great Britain, Egypt, France, and Saudi Arabia. On the day of Kuwait's invasion, President Bush immediately placed a U.S. economic embargo against Iraq, and the United Nations Security Council quickly did the same.

On November 29, 1990, the United Nations (UN) issued an ultimatum to Saddam Hussein. He was to withdraw the Iraqi military from Kuwait by January 15, 1991, or face retaliatory action from the U.S.-led coalition forces. However, it did not seem as though Hussein was planning on leaving. In order to prepare for a potential war and to keep Iraqi forces from entering Saudi Arabia, the United States positioned thousands of land, air, and naval forces in the Persian Gulf, an area which includes the countries of Bahrain, Iran, Iraq, Kuwait, Oman, Qatar, Saudi Arabia, and the United Arab Emirates. This buildup of forces in the gulf region—dubbed Operation Desert Shield by President Bush—was the largest overseas deployment of American troops since the Vietnam War (1954–1975).

By January 16, 1991, the deadline for Iraq's withdrawal from Kuwait had passed, and Saddam Hussein had ignored the UN's ultimatum.

Operation Desert Shield became Operation Desert Storm in the early morning of January 17, Baghdad time, when the U.S.-led coalition forces launched air attacks on Iraq's capital city, Baghdad, as well as other military installations within Iraq. Leaving from air bases in Saudi Arabia, England, Turkey, Egypt, and the small island of Diego Garcia in the Indian Ocean, waves of fighter planes bombed key Iraqi military targets such as missile launch sites, heavily fortified command and communications centers, airports and runways, and radar facilities. From that day on, Iraqi forces were under constant, heavy air strikes.

After five weeks of air attacks, which nearly destroyed Iraq's offensive capabilities, President Bush ordered the commencement of

This female American soldier was stationed in Damman, Saudi Arabia, in September 1990, shortly after Saddam Hussein invaded Kuwait.

the allied ground assault. With this, marine, army, and air forces moved in, pushing Iraqi forces from Kuwait. The ground war lasted just 100 hours, and it resulted in few allied casualties and a decisive victory for coalition forces. On February 27, 1991, just six weeks after the beginning of Operation Desert Storm, Kuwait City was liberated.

At the time, the Gulf War marked the largest deployment of women to combat in U.S. history. Of the 540,000 troops who were sent to the gulf region during Operation Desert Shield/Storm more than 40,000 of them were women. According to the Department of Defense, "there were approximately 26,000 Army, 3,700 Navy, 2,200 Marine, and 5,300 Air Force (USAF) women deployed."[1] The Gulf War also saw expanding roles for women. In previous wars, women had traditionally served as nurses. However, by the time of the Persian Gulf War, women were serving in almost all of the hundreds of support positions that were open to them, including administrators, engineer equipment mechanics, drivers, air traffic controllers, radio operators, and law enforcement specialists.

Though the Gulf War was a turning point for women, there were still laws and policies in effect at the time that limited their involvement. Women in the military were not allowed to serve in the front lines or in positions that would place them in direct contact with the enemy. Essentially, they were allowed to do almost anything on land, at sea, and in the air except participate in actual fighting. For some women, this meant settling for positions they would not have otherwise chosen. However, every job that was carried out was vital to the success of the war. The military relied on each person to do his or her job and function as a team. From the person who flew the fighter jet to the person who repaired it and kept it in working order, everyone was important.

The positions in which women were permitted to serve were limited in order to keep them from harm's way; however, it was clear from the beginning of the Gulf War that the line between combat and noncombat positions was a blurry one. Traditionally, frontline positions were considered to be more dangerous than support assignments. However, in the Persian Gulf War, the rear areas were no longer safe. Iraqis often fired long-range missiles into staging and supply areas that were located behind front lines. The Department of Defense stated, "Although women did not serve in

Women played a much more visible role during the Gulf War than in any preceding wars. Seven percent of the mobilized forces were female while 20 percent of the National Guard were women. Because women were still not allowed to engage in ground combat, many were posted to combat-support positions, such as operating aircraft control boards and radios.

units whose mission involved direct combat with the enemy, some women were subjected to combat."[2] Women were shot at, wounded, captured, and killed. They were also decorated for valor.

The women who fought during the Persian Gulf War joined the military for many different reasons. Some were looking for adventure, while others joined for more practical reasons such as paying for their college education. Some women joined because they wanted to follow in the footsteps of an older sibling or a parent. They may have joined for different reasons, but they were all working for one common purpose. Following are a few of the stories of the women who served their country in the air, on land, and at sea during the Persian Gulf War. Each woman has a different story, but each did her job and did it admirably.

THE WOMEN WHO SERVED IN THE AIR

Approximately 5,300 air force women were deployed for the Persian Gulf War. The laws that were in effect at the time limited the positions in which these women could serve. These laws banned women from serving on combat aircraft and ships. Nevertheless, the women of the United States Air Force played a pivotal role in the outcome of the war.

Although they were excluded from directly serving in combat missions, women flew aboard tanker aircraft, which carried out the important task of refueling bomber and fighter planes. They also served aboard transport aircraft that delivered troops, supplies, and equipment to the battlefield. Women were also permitted to serve aboard airborne warning and control systems (AWACS) aircraft. These aircraft carried out the vital task of controlling air traffic. Air force women were also assigned to air bases, where

A female helicopter pilot sorts through records and diagrams just before takeoff. Today, 99 percent of air force jobs are available to women. After the Gulf War, when it was hotly debated whether or not women should be allowed to participate in combat, the Clinton administration decided that women could serve as combat pilots.

they serviced, repaired, and armed the aircraft that were headed for combat.

Though women in the air force did not see direct combat during the Persian Gulf War, their jobs were often dangerous. The tanker aircraft in which women flew refueled fighter and bomber planes in midair during attack missions. These huge unarmed tankers were easy targets. The AWACS and the transport aircraft were also defenseless and made good targets for enemy sur-face-to-air missiles. Women were also at risk on air bases, which were frequent targets of Iraqi Scud missile attacks.

Despite the risks, the roles that the air force women played during the Persian Gulf War helped the air force to attain its goals of striking enemy targets in Kuwait and Iraq, transporting army and marine forces by air into strategic positions, and providing air support for the ground troops. With their support, the air force served to ensure a swift and decisive coalition victory by virtually devastating the Iraqi army even before the ground campaign began.

Stephanie Wells

Born May 22, 1953, Stephanie Wells became interested in aviation while in high school. Her role

U.S. SERVICEWOMEN AND THE CUSTOMS OF SAUDI ARABIA

Women in Saudi Arabia are subjected to many restrictions. They are required to follow a strict dress code, they are not permitted to drive, and they must get written permission from a male relative if they wish to travel. Though some Arabian women dress in clothes that do not cover their faces, most dress conservatively. They wear long black garments called *abayas*, which cover their bodies from their shoulders to their feet. A conservative woman might also wear face and head covers.

While stationed in Saudi Arabia, the women of the United States military were also required (to an extent) to follow the customs of the area. For example, when leaving the base, they wore abayas or clothes that, like the abayas, covered their arms and legs.

Saudi women in full chadors

(Continued on next page.)

Servicewomen also had to be accompanied by a male if they wanted to leave their bases. Some of the stores surrounding the bases were also off-limits to female personnel, while other stores simply had restrictions. Arab men often assumed that American women had "loose" morals, because women living in America do not always cover their arms and legs. Because of this, servicewomen were sometimes grabbed or forcibly kissed even when they were following the Saudi customs by covering themselves. Other U.S. women were subjected to verbal obscenities by men who were unaccustomed to independent women. On one occasion, a servicewoman left her base with her ankles showing and was caught by the Matawa, the Saudi religious police. She was struck with a camel whip around her ankles, and the blow was so forceful, it knocked her off her feet. Even during the recent Operation Iraqi Freedom, which took place in the Persian Gulf, female military personnel were forced to dress in traditional Saudi garb when going off base.

models were such heroines as Jacqueline Cochran and Amelia Earhart, both female pilots. Wells stated, "They were models of what success could be like, if one sticks to the goal."[1] Following high school, Wells entered Iowa State University and, upon the completion of a degree in meteorology in 1975, became the first female to graduate from the school's Reserve Officers Training Corps (ROTC) program.

Wells entered active duty with the air force as a weather officer. After ten years, she joined the reserves, serving part-time as a C-5 aircraft commander and full-time as a NASA staff pilot. It was at this time that tension was escalating in the gulf. Within days of President Bush's August 6, 1990, announcement that

Once a shampoo girl in a beauty parlor, Jacqueline Cochran became the first woman to break the sound barrier. To this day, many of her distance and speed records remain unbroken. She is remembered as one of the most important figures in aviation as well as in women's history.

THE C-5 GALAXY

The C-5 Galaxy is one of the largest airplanes in the world. Lockheed Martin, an advanced technology company, began designing this massive aircraft in 1963. When the first C-5 finally took to the air on June 30, 1968, many were amazed that something that big could actually fly. The aircraft is almost as long as a football field and as high as a six-story building. It also has a cargo compartment that is about the size of an eight-lane bowling alley.

Since the Vietnam War, C-5 aircraft have carried military units to locations throughout the world. They have then provided the fighting forces with the support that they have needed in order to continue fighting. During Operation Desert Storm, the C-5 provided the United States with a valuable military advantage. Along with other transport aircraft, the C-5 airlifted nearly half a million passengers and more than 577,000 tons (519,300 metric tons) of cargo from the Middle East.

troops would be sent to Saudi Arabia for
Operation Desert Shield, Wells was flying world-
wide C-5 missions while continuing her work as a
NASA staff instructor pilot. By August 29, 1990,
Wells's reserve unit, the Sixty-eighth Military
Airlift Squadron of the Military Airlift Command,
was called to active duty, becoming part of the
largest airlift operation in military history.

When Operation Desert Shield became
Operation Desert Storm in January 1991, Wells
wrote in her diary, "The attack has begun at long
last."[2] Up to this point, Wells had nervously antic-
ipated the start of the war, but, with the attack,
her attitude changed to one of "Go get 'em and
get this thing over with."[3] To her, the anxiety of
waiting for the war to begin was much worse
than actually being in it. During Operation
Desert Storm, Wells amassed 600 hours of flying
time, transporting cargo to and from the desert.
This cargo included tanks, trucks, helicopters,
missiles, medical supplies, food, and some troops.
She made twenty-two flights into dangerous hot
spots such as Saudi Arabia, the United Arab
Emirates, and Egypt.

Many of her missions were also quite long,
averaging fourteen days. Wells retired from the

On New Year's Day, Sergeant Melanie Slusher packs lunches for the pilots leaving for Saudi Arabia from Ramstein Air Base in Germany.

reserves in 1996 as a lieutenant colonel, having served twenty-one years in the military. Few military pilots could match Wells's combined experience in the air force and in NASA. She said, "I have a lifetime of experience, many hours in the air; I've traveled all over the world, and served my country faithfully and gladly."[4]

Laura Long

During the Persian Gulf War, Air Force staff sergeant Laura Long, of Sandusky, Ohio, served as a vehicle operator-dispatcher with the First Tactical Fighter Wing. Her job included making sure that the vehicles were maintained, accounting for the vehicle fleet, and organizing and directing vehicle transportation in support of missions. If there had been an opportunity for her to do so, Long would have liked to have been a combat pilot. However, due to the federal law at that time, which prohibited air force women from serving in direct combat roles, she resigned herself to the fact that she would just have to take what she could get.

As a supervisor during the war, Long felt that she should be there for everyone. During frightening Scud alerts, she worried about her drivers, wondering if they were all OK. Even though a

Upon arriving in the Middle East, Lisa Stein was asked by U.S. military officials to cover her hair and practice Judaism discreetly. Defiantly, Stein continued to practice Judaism and left her hair uncovered. As a result, she was constantly followed by Saudi religious police.

missile could have ripped through the building in which she worked at any moment, Long, who was dressed in a chemical suit and a gas mask, bravely stayed in her office making calls to her drivers instead of taking shelter in the bunkers with the rest of her colleagues.

Lisa Stein

Lisa Stein was born on March 9, 1965, in White Plains, New York. She decided to join the military because she "thought it sounded like fun and they would foot the bill for school."[5] To this end, she obtained a four-year Air Force Reserve Officer Training Corps scholarship to the University of Miami, Florida. Upon her graduation in 1987, Stein was commissioned into the United States Air Force. Following her basic training, Stein was assigned to AWACS. She accrued more than 1,800 hours of combat flight time, despite rules restricting women from flying combat missions, before being deployed to Saudi Arabia in 1990 for Operation Desert Shield.

During Operation Desert Storm, she served as a navigator on board the AWACS. These planes,

The AWAC aircraft, seen above, is a modified Boeing 707/320 commercial plane with a rotating radar dome. Its radar has a range of more than 200 miles (320 km) for low-flying targets and farther for targets flying at medium to high altitudes.

equipped with large, rotating radar discs, were used for surveillance during the war. Designed to oversee all aircraft in their operating area, AWACS identified planes as either friend or foe and then dispatched an appropriate response to deal with threats. During Operation Desert Storm, the air traffic control that was provided by AWACS, such as the one in which Lisa Stein flew, prevented catastrophic midair collisions by allied aircraft. From January 17, 1991, to March 1991, serving in such a manner, Stein accrued more than 600 combat flight hours.

During Operation Desert Storm, Iraqi troops set fire to more than 600 oil wells in Kuwait. This was a fulfillment of Saddam Hussein's promise that "if he had to be evicted from Kuwait by force, then Kuwait would be burned."[6]

These fires buried much of the Persian Gulf in a poisonous smoke. Exposure to such oil fumes damaged Stein's eyes and led to a loss of her peripheral vision. As a result of this disability, she retired from the air force, having achieved the rank of captain, in September 1992. During her military career, Stein received such decorations as the Air Medal with BOLC (Bronze Oak Leaf Cluster—this indicates that more than one of the awards it was listed with was received), the Aerial

BURNING OIL FIELDS IN KUWAIT

As Iraqi troops were evacuating Kuwait, they set fire to more than 600 oil wells. It was estimated that about 5 million gallons (18,927 kiloliters) of oil were going up in flames each day. When the war ended, 650 oil wells were still burning, and the last fire was not put out until November 1991.

An American Black Hawk flies over a burning oil well.

The burning of the oil fields caused immense amounts of smoke and oil rain to fill the desert air. Still winds then caused the plumes of smoke to drop down to the ground where the troops were. At times, the smoke was so thick that troops were only able to see about 10 feet (3 meters) in front of them. Since the Gulf War, many veterans have complained of symptoms such as shortness of breath, headaches, and memory loss. Some believe that these symptoms can be linked to the smoke and petroleum that they were exposed to while in the gulf.

Achievement Medal, the Air Force Outstanding Unit Award with BOLC, the Combat Readiness Medal, the National Defense Service Medal, and the Air Force Overseas Short Tour Ribbon.

Sherry Callahan

Air Force sergeant Sherry Callahan was an assistant maintenance crew chief with the First Tactical Fighter Wing during the Persian Gulf War. She served as a shift boss in charge of maintaining an F-15 fighter plane that she affectionately called

Daphne. "We do practically everything," she stated. "We wash it. We do maintenance on it. We take care of it, just like a personal car. Except that we can't take it home."[7]

Callahan's unit reached Saudi Arabia on the second day of Operation Desert Shield, having made a long fourteen-hour flight. After arriving in

F-15 C fighters fly over the thick, toxic smoke billowing out of Kuwait's burning oil fields. When it was certain that Iraq would lose the Gulf War, Hussein's troops torched the fields as an act of revenge and defiance. After the war, approximately 85 percent of Kuwait's oil supply was destroyed.

the gulf, Callahan labored to keep Daphne in working order. She took pride in her work, and it showed. She boasted, "It [the F-15 fighter] hasn't broken since we got here."[8] As the boss of the team that maintained the F-15 fighter, Callahan was not only responsible for the condition of the aircraft but also the safety of the pilot who flew the plane, Colonel John McBroom. A malfunctioning plane could mean disaster for its pilot. Without Callahan, Colonel McBroom, commander of the First Tactical Fighter Wing, would not have been able to carry out his duty. During Desert Storm, the F-15 fighters who operated mainly at night in order to hunt Scud missile launchers and artillery sites, "accounted for 34 of the 37 Air Force air-to-air victories."[9]

Reflecting upon her service in the Persian Gulf, Callahan said, "I learned a lot during the war, but the point that sticks with me the most is that whenever it got tough, everyone rushed to help."[10]

Sheila Chewning

Captain Sheila Chewning served on one of the air force's AWACS during the Persian Gulf War. Due to the vital role that AWACS aircraft played in the air campaign, they were often referred to as the "flying nerve centers" of Operation Desert Storm.

Communication was key to the success of the air campaign. With more than 2,000 airplanes coming and going around the clock, it was important that everyone be coordinated. AWACS made that possible. Not only did they control air traffic in the area, keeping coalition aircraft from crashing into each other, but they also spotted enemy planes and led allied aircraft to them. According to an article in *Air Force Magazine*, AWACS "played a major role in all but two of the coalition's 40 air-to-air kills of the Gulf War."[11]

As a weapons controller, Chewning utilized the sophisticated radar equipment on board the AWACS to direct U.S. fighter planes into strategic positions relative to enemy aircraft. During one of the first dogfights (aerial battles) of the war, she aided in shooting down two Iraqi fighter planes.

Also, during the first bombing raid on Baghdad, Captain Chewning orchestrated the downing of two Russian-built Iraqi MiG-29s by U.S. F-15 fighters. It was a tense moment. After directing the U.S. fighters in the attack, Chewning anxiously listened to her radio as the fighter pilots located the MiGs, fired upon them, and finally announced that they had shot enemy aircraft down. "The minutes between hearing the pilots

Anti-aircraft fire blazes across Baghdad's night sky as U.S. planes fly overhead in an early morning attack on January 18, 1991. The United States began a major air attack against Iraq on January 17. More than 1,000 warplanes bombarded Iraq every day with smart bombs, daisy cutters, cluster bombs, and cruise missiles.

say 'contact,' 'engaged,' and then 'splashed' seemed like a long, long time,"[12] Chewning recalled. However, it was times like these for which she was trained. "When that happened [bringing down an enemy plane], we really felt like we were doing our jobs."[13]

THE WOMEN WHO SERVED ON LAND

During the Gulf War, the task of the army and marine forces was to defend Saudi Arabia from invasion and to push the Iraqi army out of Kuwait. When the ground campaign began in the early hours of February 24, 1991, most of the Iraqi troops fled at the mere sight of the U.S. ground troops. Those that did not were either captured or killed. The ground war lasted for only 100 hours, or four days, and with its end came the end of the Persian Gulf War.

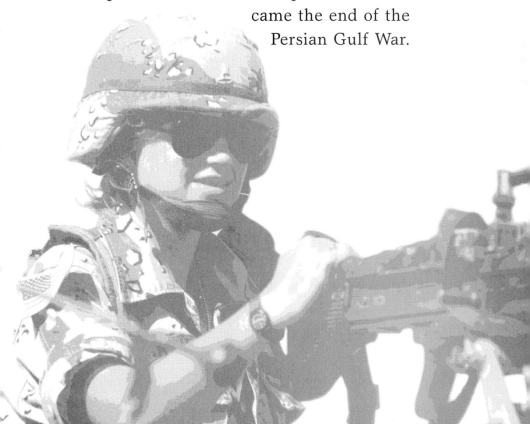

Of all the women deployed in the Gulf War, the number of those in the army—approximately 26,000—far exceeded the other branches of the military. Women served in important roles, such as tank mechanics, keeping the tanks in working order; truck drivers, hauling important equipment and fuel to frontline units; and guards, protecting bases from terrorist attacks and watching prisoners of war.

The army differed from the other branches of the military in that, while the air force, navy, and marines had a federal law prohibiting women from serving in direct combat roles, the army only had internal policy, which paralleled those laws. These policies forbade women from serving in the front lines and in units that participated in direct combat. However, due to the sophistication of the weaponry used during the Gulf War, it was not often clear where the front line was. Long-range Iraqi artillery could easily reach women who were serving in noncombat units or in units in the rear. Noncombat units were fired upon and often had casualties. Support positions in which the women served also often took them into the thick of the battle as they followed the forward units that they were supporting.

Carol Barkalow

Carol Barkalow was born on December 26, 1958, in Neptune, New Jersey. Barkalow planned to join the military after graduating from her upstate New

WEST POINT OPENS TO WOMEN

In 1975, President Gerald Ford signed a law requiring West Point, as well as two other military schools, Annapolis and the Air Force Academy, to open their doors to women. West Point began admitting women in 1976, and the first 327 female cadets began their education that fall. The first coed class at West Point graduated in 1980, seeing 217 of the original 327 women completing the program. It had taken an act of Congress to open the United States military academies to women, and not everyone was pleased about the decision. However, many women have succeeded, showing that they are capable of handling challenging physical and military courses.

The West Point class of 1980 was the first to include female graduates. Although the class of 1980 graduated only half of the initial 327 women who entered, more than 1,000 women had graduated by 1991. Women are now approximately 15 percent of the Corps of Cadets. Above is the class of 1997.

York high school. As her graduation neared, Barkalow was convinced to attend West Point by a guidance counselor who stopped her as she cut through the school's guidance office. At the time, she did not even know where West Point was, but the guidance counselor informed her that they were accepting women, so she applied. Barkalow was admitted, and on July 7, 1976, at age seventeen, she entered the first class at West Point to include women.

At West Point, Barkalow and her classmates experienced grueling physical training and merciless hazing practices. However, these experiences only increased her determination to succeed.

After graduating from West Point, Barkalow worked for a while in air defense in Germany but found that there were few positions open to women. Barkalow decided to switch to a career in transportation, and when the Persian Gulf War began, she volunteered as a transportation specialist.

During the war, she served as a combat support officer, commanding a truck company that used light and medium weight vehicles. There were more than 70

A yearbook picture of Carol Barkalow shows her proudly smiling after she completed her training at Fort Benning, Georgia, in 1978. Barkalow recalls that in order to qualify for airborne service, she had to jump out of a plane five times, falling 1,250 feet (381 m).

vehicles and 140 soldiers. Of the men in her unit, Barkalow said: "There was hesitation on their part, not knowing what to expect. But it didn't take them long to discover that I was committed to taking care of them. After they saw that, they didn't have a problem. The overriding factor is professionalism."[1]

As part of a support unit, Barkalow's company provided assistance for the lead combat brigade in the Twenty-fourth Infantry Division.

In the early, scary hours of the war, Barkalow's unit moved into Iraq right along with the Twenty-fourth Infantry Division. Though not technically allowed to fight in the front line, it seemed to Barkalow that the line between the front and rear was blurred due to the sophistication and long ranges of the weaponry that was being used. "Before the ground war started, we were 15 kilometers [9.3 miles] south of the border," she stated. "When the Iraqis lobbed artillery to see where we were, I could feel the vibrations in my chest from the explosions."[2] At times, Barkalow felt as though support units, such as hers, were at even more risk, because they lacked the firepower to properly defend themselves. However, Barkalow said of her time in the gulf, "We [the men and women of the army] really pulled together in conditions that were worse than horrible."[3] The decorations Barkalow has received include the Meritorious Service Medal and the National Defense Service Medal.

Ora Jane Williams

Ora Jane "O. J." Williams stumbled upon the military when, while attending a movie with a friend, she ran into an army recruiter who was handing out literature. Williams, who at the time was teaching high school home economics and science in Natchez, Mississippi, was looking for a change in career and thought the army looked interesting. Eight months later, in 1972, Williams began her career with the army and became a lieutenant by direct commission. Prior to the Persian Gulf War, Williams worked as a protocol officer, an administrative supply officer, a field service company commander, and a logistician. She also served overseas in Germany and Korea, and attended the Command and General Staff College in Fort Leavenworth, Kansas.

Forty-nine-year-old Williams arrived in Saudi Arabia for Operation Desert Shield in mid-August 1990, having left behind a twelve-year-old adopted son. At the time of her deployment, Williams was a lieutenant colonel with eighteen years of army service under her belt. During the war, she served as commanding officer of the Second Material Management Center, a battalion-size logistics management unit. Her unit was responsible for the computerized requisition of supplies for the Twenty-fourth Infantry Division (Mechanized), the 101st Airborne Division, and the Eighty-second Airborne Division. Each day, they handled tens of thousands of requests from these combat divisions for important items such as repair parts, clothing, ammo, food, and other supplies. These items were then obtained from either Saudi Arabia or the United States. Though she did not directly engage in combat during the Persian Gulf War, the service that Williams provided as a logistician was vital. Without her, troops would not have had the supplies that they needed in order to carry out their jobs.

Stacy Jalowitz-Welter

Stacy Jalowitz-Welter was born on July 25, 1971, in Hayward, Wisconsin. She was the youngest of three girls born to Jim and Sandy Jalowitz. She attended Hayward High School, where she participated in sports such as softball, volleyball, and basketball. Shortly before graduating from high school, Jalowitz-Welter enlisted in the Army National Guard, following in the footsteps of her older sister, Sue, who had joined in 1986. After graduating high school in 1989, she attended basic training in Fort Jackson, South Carolina, followed by advanced individual training in Fort Sam, Texas. She then returned to Wisconsin, where she began classes at the University of Wisconsin, Eau Claire, in the fall of 1990. It was during her freshman year at the University of Wisconsin that Jalowitz-Welter's unit, including her sister, was activated. She and her sister left for Saudi Arabia on January 11, 1991, and arrived there two days later.

While in the gulf, Jalowitz-Welter served as a pharmacy technician in the Thirteenth Evacuation Hospital. Her job included tending to casualties and guarding Iraqi soldiers that had been taken as prisoners. Initially, Jalowitz-Welter lived with her sister on the U.S. air base in Dhahran in an apartment that overlooked the Persian Gulf. Later, her unit transferred to a desert location, just miles south of the Iraqi border. Here, Jalowitz-Welter's unit set up a 400-bed

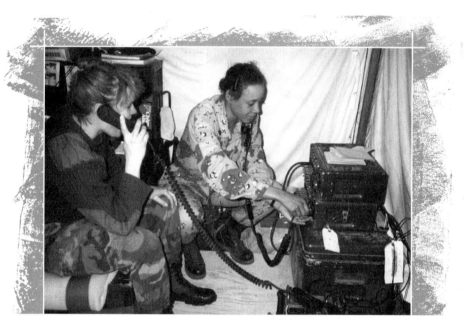

Navy hospital corpsmen set up a communications station at a field hospital during Operation Desert Storm on February 27, 1991, in Saudi Arabia. Although U.S. troops were in Saudi Arabia partly as protection for the Saudis themselves, their presence—and their use of women soldiers—upset some fundamentalist clerics, who saw them as invaders.

hospital that was used to treat wounded soldiers. While continuing to do her job, Jalowitz-Welter experienced frequent sandstorms and terrifying Scud alerts, which took place at all hours of the day. After having served for three and a half months in Saudi Arabia, Jalowitz-Welter, along with her unit, flew back to the United States on April 26, 1991. Upon her return home, Jalowitz-Welter returned to the University of Wisconsin,

Eau Claire, in order to complete her education. She graduated in 1995 with a bachelor of arts degree in accounting and business administration.

Barbara Bates

During the Persian Gulf War, Barbara Bates served as a meteorologist. Bates was part of a forward-based self-propelled howitzer artillery unit of the Twenty-fourth Infantry Division (Mechanized). She was the only female in the unit, serving with more than 700 artillerymen. As a meteorologist, Bates provided readouts on the local temperature, winds, and other conditions. Though she had a noncombat specialty, the information that Bates obtained was vital to the combat unit that she supported.

Weather was a major concern during Operation Desert Shield and Operation Desert Storm. Rain, clouds, and sandstorms can determine the success or failure of a military operation. Even the most well-equipped army is subject to the limits that terrain, climate, and weather place on it. Therefore, it is very important that meteorologists, such as Bates, study the weather during wartime.

Most of the rainfall in the gulf region occurs during the months of November and April. The winter months are from December through March. The early-winter months are characterized by fog, rain, and clouds, the cloudier months being December and January. Such rainy and cloudy weather is not conducive to bombing raids or reconnaissance missions. Therefore, it is important that such missions are planned around information, such as that provided by Bates during the Persian Gulf War.

Heavy winds, which can cause large sandstorms, are typical in the months of January and February. This season is called the Shammal, which means "north," and describes the winds responsible for the storms. Sandstorms interfere with laser-guided weapons and can potentially clog engines and wear down helicopter blades. The Shammal is also characterized by heavy fog that can make aircraft flight difficult. U.S. and coalition forces experienced sandstorms while in the gulf. However, when predicted by meteorologists, such as Bates, the military was able to plan around these storms.

Between the months of February and April, high winds averaging 35 to 45 miles per hour (56 to 72 kilometers per hour), stir up sandstorms. This is followed by the haboob, a Bedouin word meaning "the worst possible combination of things," so named because of the fast-moving thunderstorms that move along within the sand-storm. Weather like this keeps military radar equipment—which is used to determine the position,

In Iraq, American soldiers had to learn how to dig into the ground to make shelters from sandstorms and enemy ground attacks. One of the biggest trials for American soldiers during the Gulf War was adapting to Iraq's harsh desert environment.

size, and velocity of distant objects—from working properly. With the information that Bates provided during the Persian Gulf War, troops were able to make decisions that made the difference between wasted ammunition and good shots.

Cynthia Mosley

Cynthia Mosley, a 1984 summa cum laude graduate of Alabama Agricultural and Mechanical University, spent seven months in the gulf region during Operation Desert Shield/Storm. She served as the commander of Alpha Company, the Twenty-fourth Support Battalion (Forward), Twenty-fourth Infantry Division (Mechanized). This battalion was deployed farther forward than any other American supply battalion in Saudi Arabia. Of the 400 troops in this battalion, nearly a quarter were women.

Mosley's 100-person unit supplied tank crews and infantry with everything from medicine and food to fuel, ammunition, and spare parts. Mosley's company even had to refuel the forward brigades when all of them ran out of fuel. Without that precious fuel, these brigades would have been stranded, unable to perform their duties. "We were supporting not only the brigade we were assigned," she recalled, "but everybody forward during that particular time in the war."[4] Mosley's unit drove into Iraq just six hours after the fighting, and the memories of the horrific sights she saw still haunt her. However, with resolve she stated, "You just learn to live with it and continue on."[5] For her efforts in the Gulf War, Mosley received the Bronze Star for meritorious service in combat.

Gianna Nenna (Fibres) Church

Gianna Nenna Church, nicknamed Gee Gee, was born on March 12, 1960, in Tucson, Arizona. Church joined the air force in 1978 and served for five years. After taking a four-year break from the military, she then joined the army in 1987. During the Persian Gulf War, Church served as a petroleum supply specialist in Saudi Arabia. Units that were scattered across the desert relied on her, and the convoys of fuel trucks that she drove with, to supply them with fuel. This meant that Church had to travel day and night, getting little or no sleep.

The terrain that the fuel trucks had to travel upon to get to those who needed fuel often presented them with difficulty. To do her job, Church had to drive over rocky land covered with boulders, hills, and sand.

On one occasion, while traveling across some particularly difficult terrain, Church and several other soldiers found themselves stuck in the desert with two flat tires. While stranded in the sand, they were fired upon by Iraqi tanks, small arms, and M203 grenade launchers. One of Church's companions, as well as her truck, was hit. As Church and her companions ran up a hill, they were suddenly blown to the ground. Church was able to escape with her life, but it is an experience that she will never forget.

Church has received many decorations throughout her military career, including the National Defense Service Medal, the Southwest Asia Service Medal, the Army Commendation Medal, and the Army Achievement Medal.

Phoebe Ann Jeter

Phoebe Ann Jeter was born on February 21, 1964, in Chester, South Carolina. Jeter, who, during the Gulf War, became the first woman to shoot down Scuds, had decided to join the army "for some adventure."[6] In her three years in the army before going to war, Jeter had practiced destroying surface-to-surface missiles for countless hours. The

Lieutenant Phoebe Jeter stands guard over the remains of a fallen Scud missile in Saudi Arabia in 1991. Jeter was praised for her ability to keep a cool head when under attack. Of her desire to be a soldier, she said, "I thought everybody grew up playing war."

Persian Gulf War, however, presented her with the opportunity to put her training into action.

During the war, Jeter was in charge of a Patriot missile control team in Riyadh, Saudi Arabia. Her all-male platoon had the task of identifying incoming Scuds, calculating their speed and locations, and then shooting them down with Patriot missiles, U.S. antimissile missiles. "I was in charge of the van that is the engagement control center—where we fire [the Patriot missiles] from. I was the commander inside the van. I was in charge of everything that happened inside that van. It was my responsibility,"[7] Jeter recalled.

Jeter's most memorable experience from the Gulf War came on January 21, 1990. As a Scud alert sounded, Jeter learned that Scuds were headed toward the base in which she worked. Through her gas mask, she shouted commands to her tactical control assistant, ordering the launch of thirteen Patriot missiles in all. When it was all over, the Patriots that Jeter had fired had destroyed two Scuds. For her competence and level-headedness under fire, Jeter became the first woman to receive the Army Commendation Medal in the gulf. Other decorations that Jeter received include the Army Achievement Medal, the National Defense Service Medal, the Southwest Asia Service Medal, the Army Service Ribbon, and the Army Overseas Service Ribbon.

THE WOMEN WHO SERVED AT SEA

3

During the Persian Gulf War, the United States Navy had the task of stopping Iraqi trade, protecting friendly ships, and launching an attack on Iraq. Many of the troops, ammunition, and supplies that were needed in the gulf were brought there by navy ships. Navy ships also fired missiles on Baghdad and Kuwait, opening the way for allied ground forces during the ground war. The first shot fired in Operation Desert Storm was, in fact, fired from a navy ship. Many planes were also launched from the decks of navy ships.

Approximately 3,700 navy women were deployed for the Persian Gulf War. Though women were kept from serving on combat ships, they played a crucial role in the contribution that the navy made to the war. Women served on hospital ships, providing medical care to thousands of military personnel. They also served aboard ships that provided ammunition, repair, and essential supplies

A Tomahawk missile sails across the sky heading for its target. The Tomahawk is a long-range cruise missile that travels at approximately 547 mph (880 kmh). During the Gulf War, coalition forces launched 288 Tomahawks.

to the entire American fleet. Women also served ashore in fleet hospitals, in construction battalions, and in several other support positions.

The support vessels on which the U.S. Navy women sailed were not out of harm's way. These ships often went without the protection of the fleet and were vulnerable to floating mines and Iraqi missiles. However, despite these risks, no navy women participated in combat, either directly or indirectly.

Brenda Holdener

Brenda Holdener was born on November 28, 1960, in East Saint Louis, Illinois. While in high school, she decided to join the navy. Following her 1978 high school graduation, Holdener received an NROTC scholarship to a state university. She graduated from the university with a degree in construction engineering management and was commissioned into the United States Navy in June 1985.

Holdener served for two years as a general unrestricted line officer, assigned to the Naval Manpower Engineering Center in San Diego before being selected for the naval aviation program. She received her wings in July 1988 and was detailed to fly the H-46 Sea Knight, a helicopter used for such purposes as moving troops and equipment, medical evacuation, firefighting, heavy construction, and search and rescue.

Holdener served briefly in Norfolk, Virginia, before being deployed to Saudi Arabia for the Persian Gulf War. During the war, she served as Detachment Seven officer in charge aboard the USNS *Sirius* (T-AFS 8). The *Sirius* is a combat stores ship that delivers goods to combat ships with the help of the two H-46 Sea Knight helicopters that are assigned to it. As one of the pilots of these helicopters, Holdener carried out the important task of ferrying essential supplies such as fresh food, clothing, repair parts, and mail to U.S. ships on the Red Sea during the Persian Gulf War.

The H-46 Sea Knight helicopters, like the ones in which Holdener flew, have served the navy and Marine Corps in all combat and peacetime environments. These aircraft fly day and night in any weather, faithfully supplying operations that take place on the water and on land. On being a woman in the navy, Holdener stated, "We're not without the guys who don't want us there, but that just makes women work harder and want to be there."[1]

Holdener's personal decorations include the Meritorious Service Medal, a Navy Achievement Medal with one gold star, a Navy Commendation Medal with two gold stars, and several unit and operational awards.

Sandra (Villarreal) Hormiga

Petty Officer Sandra Hormiga was born on November 21, 1964, in Houston. Hormiga, who served in the United States Navy from August 1987 to August 1991, was one of many Hispanic women in the navy who were deployed overseas during Operation Desert Shield/Storm. During the war, she served aboard the ship USS *McKee*, a submarine tender that provided support to submarines and surface combatants. Hormiga, along with the rest of the crew of the USS *McKee*, served to provide everything that a submarine might need, from repair materials to medical supplies.

Throughout the Gulf War, there were serious concerns that Saddam Hussein would use chemical or biological weapons on coalition forces. As the USS *McKee* made its way to the Middle East, its crew performed many drills in preparation of possible chemical attacks. One day, while performing a general quarters drill, it suddenly dawned on

Hormiga that one of these drills could turn out to be real. She realized, "We were no longer 'just doing drills,' we were practicing saving our own lives."[2] From then on, Hormiga treated each drill as if it were an actual chemical attack. Though allied forces were prepared, they were not faced with any chemical or biological attacks.

The USS *Louisville* surfaces in the Persian Gulf, 1992. The *Louisville* was the first submarine to fire its Tomahawk missiles. During the Gulf War, only twelve Tomahawks were launched from submarines.

CHEMICAL AND BIOLOGICAL WARFARE

Chemical and biological weapons are weapons of mass destruction, which are, by definition, capable of easily killing thousands of people. Any manufactured chemical that is used to kill people is considered a chemical weapon. Biological weapons use viruses, bacteria, or toxins that come from bacteria. The first chemical weapons were used in World War I. Following this, it was decided that these weapons, whose effects cannot be predicted or controlled, were too dangerous. A treaty, called the Geneva Protocol, was put into place in 1925. Since then, it has been signed by most of the nations of the world. However, the protocol has several loopholes, including the fact that it does not prohibit the manufacture of or the threat to use these weapons. It also does not mention punishment for violators of the protocol.

During the Gulf War, the United States military feared the use of Iraqi chemical and biological weapons because it was known that Iraq had done extensive research on these topics. The most likely way that chemical or biological weapons would be used on the battlefield would be through distribution by exploding bombs or missiles. During the Gulf War, U.S. military personnel wore gas masks and completely covered their skin when such attacks were deemed possible.

In preparation for such attacks, protective masks and clothing were issued to the troops. Medical personnel were also trained in the decontamination and treatment of potential victims.

Preparing for the worst, American troops practice chemical treatment in the Saudi desert on February 20, 1991.

Bonnie Burnham Potter

In 1968, Bonnie Burnham Potter earned her bachelor's degree in animal science from the University of California at Davis. She later went on to receive a doctor of medicine degree from the St. Louis University School of Medicine in 1975. Potter completed her internship and residency in internal medicine at the Naval Regional Medical Center in Oakland, California. She worked at the Naval Regional Medical Center as chief resident from 1978 to 1979 and then continued there as a staff internist and residency training officer until 1983.

In August 1990, Potter was deployed in support of Operations Desert Shield and Desert Storm, and she remained in the gulf region until April 1991. She served on board the USNS *Comfort*, a naval hospital ship, as head of medical services.

The USNS *Comfort* was called up for duty in support of Operation Desert Shield on August 9, 1990. On August 11, the hospital ship departed from its home port in Baltimore and sailed toward the Persian Gulf, arriving on September 8. During Operation Desert Storm, the *Comfort* was positioned very close to Kuwait, just off the coast of Saudi Arabia. The *Comfort* shared these waters with the only other U.S. Navy hospital ship, the USNS *Mercy*. During its eight-month deployment, the *Comfort* traveled more than 35,000 miles (56,327 km), consuming nearly 3 million gallons

(11,356 kl) of fuel. While in the gulf, the staff on board this hospital ship saw more than 8,000 outpatients and performed 337 surgical procedures.

This 1,000-bed hospital ship was equipped with operating rooms, intensive care units, and advanced diagnostic equipment. The medical staff on board the ship treated more than 8,000 patients and was prepared, if it had been necessary, to treat servicemen injured by chemical and biological weapons.

Following the Persian Gulf War, Potter continued her service in the United States Navy. She served in such positions as commander at the National Naval Medical Center in Bethesda, Maryland; as chief of the medical corps at the Bureau of Medicine and Surgery in Washington, D.C.; and as fleet surgeon for the U.S. Atlantic Fleet. Potter was promoted to rear admiral in 1997 and received her second admiral star in 2000.

Rear Admiral Potter's military decorations include the Defense Meritorious Service Medal, the Meritorious Medal with gold star, the Defense Superior Service Medal, the Legion of Merit with gold star, the Navy Achievement Medal, the Navy Commendation Medal, the Combat Action Ribbon, and several other campaign awards.

Rosemary (Bryant) Mariner

Rosemary Mariner was born on April 2, 1953, in
Harlingen, Texas. She joined the navy in 1973,
becoming one of the first eight women to enter
military pilot training. In 1974, Mariner became the
first woman to fly a tactical jet aircraft when she
piloted the A-4E/L Skyhawk, a jet-powered light-
attack bomber. She made history again, just a year

later, when she became the first female pilot to fly in a frontline combat aircraft, the A-7E Corsair II.

One of the major concerns that the navy's battle groups faced throughout the Persian Gulf War was

The USNS *Comfort*, a hospital ship, was a useful component of the American forces during Operation Desert Shield. The *Comfort* stretches 894 feet (272 m) and employs 300 military personnel and 61 civilians. The *Comfort* is one of the 35 ships in the Naval Fleet Auxiliary Force.

antiship missiles from Iran and Iraq. During Operation Desert Storm, Mariner commanded an electric warfare squadron. Electronic warfare is military action that utilizes electromagnetic energy to obstruct, damage, or destroy an enemy's electronic equipment. It also involves warfare that uses electromagnetic energy as the destructive mechanism of weapons, such as laser beams. Electronic warfare also serves to immediately recognize and provide protection against an enemy's use of such energy.

Mariner's squadron, Tactical Electronic Warfare Squadron Thirty-four, was a training squadron that served to prepare battle groups to respond to antiship missiles. During training exercises, Mariner's squadron played an adversary role, acting as the enemy against coalition forces. By utilizing the equipment and tactics in the same way that a potential enemy would, Mariner's squadron helped to prepare allied forces for an actual attack. This was an important job, because it gave the battle groups the skills and confidence that they needed in order to handle real-life situations.

In 1997, Mariner retired from the navy as a captain, having served twenty-four years as a naval

On March 22, 2002, Photographer's Mate 3rd Class Jayme Pastoric took this picture of the USS *John C. Stennis* preparing to launch an S-3B Viking fighter jet.

aviator. During her time in the military, she logged more than 3,500 flight hours in fifteen different types of naval aircraft and made seventeen landings on aircraft carriers. Mariner now works at the Center for the Study for War and Society at the University of Tennessee in Knoxville.

THE WOMEN WHO WERE HELD AS POWs

4

During the Persian Gulf War, two female United States military personnel were taken as prisoners of war (POWs). They were the first American female POWs since World War II, when eighty-eight women were held prisoner in Germany, Japan, and the Philippines.

Both were serving in the army but were captured under different circumstances. One was taken when her truck became stuck in the desert, and the other after the helicopter in which she was flying was shot down.

Navy nurses held as POWs for three years in a Luzon internment camp in the Philippines speak with Admiral Thomas C. Kinkaid shortly after their release in 1945. Starvation, torture, and disease were common hardships for prisoners of war in Japanese camps during World War II.

Before it was confirmed that women had been taken as prisoners, experts began speculating about how female POWs would be treated. While some believed that any woman held prisoner would be subjected to unspeakable horrors, others believed that women captured in this war would be treated humanely, in light of Islamic law, which states that killing a women is a serious crime. Both women stated that their captors had essentially treated them well. However, although both women initially claimed that they had not been sexually assaulted, one of the women later revealed that she had been.

Melissa (Rathbun-Nealy) Coleman

Melissa Coleman, the only child of Leo and Joan Rathbun, grew up in Grand Rapids, Michigan. Coleman attended Creston High School, where one out of ten students joined the junior ROTC program. The ROTC was so popular at the school that a firing range and special classrooms were built in order to accommodate the program. Here, Coleman learned to march, read maps, and shoot a rifle. Coleman graduated from high school in 1988 and joined the army shortly thereafter. She was seeking adventure and also figured that the army would be a good way to help her earn money for college. Following her enlistment in the army, Coleman was stationed at Fort Bliss, Texas. As a member of the 233rd Transportation Company, she was trained to drive a heavy equipment transporter, a large truck used to transport tanks and

Melissa Coleman grips her mother's hand as she listens to an encouraging speech by Secretary of Defense Dick Cheney. Coleman and other prisoners of war were released in March 1991. At the time of this photo, Coleman's last name was Rathbun-Nealy, due to a brief marriage early in her career.

other heavy equipment. Coleman served in the army for two and a half years before she was deployed for Operation Desert Shield.

When Coleman was sent to Saudi Arabia in October 1990, she made it clear that she did not want to be left out of the action. According to Coleman's father, "She told her supervisor that she didn't want to be stuck behind a desk. She wanted to do what she was trained to do."[1] During the war, Coleman was definitely doing what she was trained to do as she hauled tanks to the front lines. She was also doing what she was trained to do on January 20, 1991, when she was captured by Iraqi soldiers while carrying supplies to the front lines near the border of Kuwait.

On that date, more than three weeks before the 100-hour ground war began, Coleman was driving in a two-truck convoy when it made a wrong turn. The group ended up accidentally crossing the border from Saudi Arabia into Kuwait, the country being invaded by Sadaam Hussein's Iraqi troops. The two trucks found themselves surrounded by Iraqi tanks, armored patrol vehicles, and troops that were moving into the city of Khafji, Saudi Arabia. The trucks were fired upon, but Coleman was unable to escape when her vehicle stalled. "All of the sudden, we hear gunfire, and I just jumped on the floor,"[2] Coleman

THE 1949 GENEVA CONVENTION AND THE TREATMENT OF POWs

There are currently four Geneva Conventions. These documents were written in an effort to make warfare more compassionate. The original Geneva Convention was drafted in 1864, but it was replaced by the current four conventions in 1949, which were adopted in response to the atrocities of World War II. During World War II, millions of prisoners were killed or died from ill treatment while in the hands of foreigners.

The 1949 convention states that POWs must be treated humanely. Any action or act of negligence that causes the death of a POW, or endangers his or her health, is a violation to the convention. POWs are also to be removed, as soon as possible, from any area in which fighting is taking place and are to be protected from physical and mental harm at all times. Therefore, POWs are not to be used as human shields. This also means that captors should protect their prisoners from any kind of assault.

POWs must also be provided with adequate food, shelter, and medical care. Captors must also allow their prisoners to be visited by the International Committee of the Red Cross, which checks the condition and treatment of the POWs. The convention also prohibits captors from forcing POWs to reveal information. POWs are required only to give their name, rank, serial number, and date of birth. Under no circumstances are they to be tortured, either physically or mentally. POWs are also entitled to keep their personal property and protective gear, unless these articles pose a security issue.

---

recalled. Both Coleman and her passenger, David Lockett, were injured. She had suffered a shot to the arm, and Lockett had taken several bullets to the chest. They were soon surrounded by ten to fifteen armed Iraqi soldiers and taken prisoner.

The two were taken to Basra, a military command center and a key port city located just north of Kuwait, and then to a prison in Baghdad where they received medical treatment. On January 20, the Iraqis stated that allied POWs would be used as human shield against American air attacks on their military sites. This meant that the Iraqi military would move allied POWs to locations that were likely to be bombed by coalition forces in order to deter them from making such attacks. In his despair, Coleman's father wrote a letter to Saddam Hussein, pleading for his daughter's release.

On March 3, 1991, Coleman and Lockett were released, along with four other American POWs, as part of the first prisoner exchange. Soon after her release, Coleman stated that she had been treated well by Iraqi soldiers. Though some prisoners had reported being beaten, starved, and held in solitary confinement, Coleman said that she had been fed three meals a day, had had access to the prison's courtyard, and had been allowed to walk freely down the hall from her cell to a bathroom. "I was just alone, I was by myself, and I had to rely on myself and my mind,"[3] Coleman recalled. Coleman passed the time by singing, talking to herself, and recalling childhood memories.

After her release, Coleman returned to her post in El Paso, Texas, and married Michael Coleman, a fellow Gulf War veteran who had proposed to her before the war. In 1993, Coleman left the military and moved to San Antonio, Texas, where she now lives. The first U.S. servicewoman imprisoned by enemies since World War II, Coleman was awarded the Purple Heart, the National Defense Service Medal, and the Prisoner of War Medal.

During the Persian Gulf War, the U.S.-led coalition forces held more than 80,000 Iraqis as prisoners of war, all of whom were treated in accordance with the 1949 Geneva Convention.

Rhonda Cornum

Rhonda Cornum was born in Dayton, Ohio. A self-proclaimed tomboy, Cornum played with frogs and learned how to shoot a gun from her grandfather. Cornum came from a long line of strong women, like her great-grandmother, who had been a pilot in the 1930s. Having completed all the requirements of graduation early, Cornum graduated from high school in 1971, after her junior year. She then attended Wilmington College in Ohio for two years on a full tuition scholarship before transferring to Cornell University in New York. Cornum graduated from Cornell with a bachelor of science degree in microbiology and genetics and then remained at the school, pursuing a doctorate in biochemistry.

The army was the farthest thing from Cornum's mind when, while presenting research on amino acids at a conference, an army officer approached her. The lieutenant colonel from the Letterman Army Institute of Research at the Presidio of San Francisco was looking for someone to do amino

Honored as a prisoner of war during Operation Desert Storm, a solemn-looking Rhonda Cornum attends a welcome home ceremony at Andrews Air Force Base in Maryland. Cornum was one of many POWs to be publicly honored at the ceremony.

acid metabolic research. Needing a job, Cornum accepted. In 1978, after earning a Ph.D. in nutrition and biochemistry from Cornell, she signed on with the army.

At first, Cornum had signed on to be a scientist, not a soldier, but she was soon enthusiastic about being in the military. She earned the esteemed Expert Field Medical Badge by marching 12 miles (19 km) with a 35-pound (16-kilogram) backpack, and for her work parachuting out of planes, she received the Airborne Badge.

In 1982, Cornum decided to go to medical school, and she enrolled in the military's Uniformed Services University in Bethesda, Maryland. While in medical school, Cornum met her future husband, Kory, who convinced her to attend the army's aviation medicine basic course. Here, Cornum learned how to be a flight surgeon— a doctor who cares for pilots. In 1986, Cornum graduated from medical school in the top third of her class and then went to work at Fort Rucker in Alabama. It was here that Cornum was working when the Persian Gulf War began.

Cornum was deployed to Saudi Arabia for Operation Desert Shield in August 1990. She served as a flight surgeon for the Army's 229th Attack Helicopter Battalion. As a flight surgeon, Cornum took care of the medical needs of more than 300 soldiers. During attack missions, her job was to fly behind the Apache attack helicopters and, if one was shot down, to rescue the pilots before they were captured. On February 27, 1991, the last day of the four-day ground war, Cornum answered an emergency call to retrieve an injured air force captain, Bill Andrews, who had been shot down behind enemy lines. While she and seven other crew members were flying in a Black Hawk search-and-rescue helicopter over a seemingly empty desert, they were suddenly fired upon by antiaircraft guns. Though the Black Hawk gunners fired back furiously, the helicopter's back end was blown off, and they crashed into the sand. Five of

the eight crew members died as a result of the crash. Thirty-six-year-old Cornum suffered two broken arms, a shattered knee, and a bullet to her right shoulder. Cornum, along with the two other surviving crewmen, was taken captive, becoming one of the war's twenty-three POWs.

Soon after her capture, Cornum felt sure that she would be killed as she and another POW were forced to kneel while rifles were pointed to their heads. She recalled, "One of the guards spoke a few words of English and he seemed to say, 'Kill them! Kill them!'"[4] They were not killed but were, instead, moved around to several locations, where they were interrogated. The first twenty-four hours of her captivity were probably the worst. Cornum was most angered when one of her captors stole her wedding ring. Then, as she was being transported to Basra in the back of a pickup truck, Cornum was sexually assaulted by an Iraqi soldier. However, other Iraqi soldiers were kind to Cornum.

Pictured at left is a Black Hawk combat assault helicopter. The Black Hawk was first flown in October 1974. A heavyweight aircraft, it can hold up to eleven fully equipped soldiers, survive most weather conditions, and withstand hits from 23mm shells.

Cornum was helpless, due to her arm injuries. Several soldiers helped her to use the bathroom, respectfully averting their eyes. They also fed her bread, water, and vegetables by hand. Cornum was even offered tea. When she was finally taken to a hospital, doctors X-rayed and cast her arms and removed the bullet from her shoulder. Grateful for having made it to a hospital, Cornum sang to herself and prayed, "Thank you, Lord. Thank you, Lord, for getting me here."[5] Finally, after eight days of captivity, Cornum was released, along with fifteen other American POWs, on March 6, 1991.

Following the Persian Gulf War, Cornum was made a colonel and, in the mid-1990s, she commanded an army medical unit in Tuzla during the U.S. operation in Bosnia. In 1992, Cornum wrote a book, entitled *She Went to War: The Rhonda Cornum Story*, in which she tells the story of her life and her time spent as a POW.

Today, Cornum is an army colonel, studying at the National War College in Washington, D.C. For her service during the Persian Gulf War, Cornum received the Purple Heart, the Prisoner of War Medal, and the National Defense Service Medal. Cornum said of the POWs held during the

2003 war in the gulf, Operation Iraqi Freedom, "They can survive this and come out of it OK. I did . . . I'm fine today."[6]

THE WOMEN WHO GAVE THEIR LIVES

5

Never before had so many women been as close to the front line as they were in the Persian Gulf War. Laws and policies at the time excluded women from serving in combat units, such as navy destroyers and army infantry. However, these restrictions did not keep them out of harm's way. Though they were in support positions, the women who fought in the Gulf War clearly faced the same dangers as the men. Twenty-one women were wounded in action, and sixteen others suffered nonbattle injuries. Of the fourteen women who

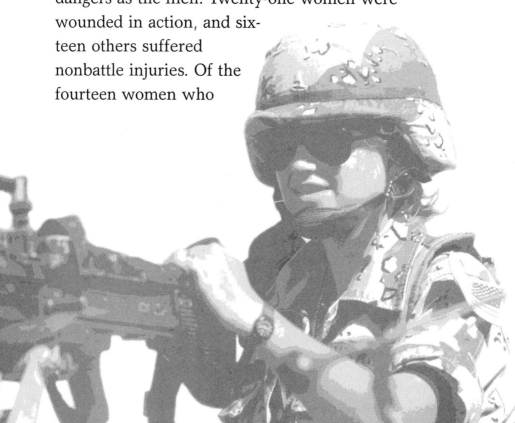

died in the Gulf War, five were considered by the military to have been killed in action. One of these women, Marie Rossi-Cayton, was killed in a helicopter crash, three others died in a Scud missile attack, and one was killed when a mine exploded.

Tatiana (Khaghani) Dees

Tatiana Dees was born on July 25, 1956, in Iran. Dees, an army staff sergeant, served with the

This is a memorial to all the soldiers who served in Desert Storm from Columbia County, New York. As female soldiers are permitted to take on more combat duties, they also take on the risks of death and injury that all soldiers face.

Ninety-second Military Police Battalion, which was based in Germany. Dees became the first female noncombat fatality of Desert Shield when, on January 7, 1991, she fell from a pier in Dhahran, Iraq, and drowned. Dees had been patrolling the pier in the port city of Ad Dammam when she noticed an unknown person taking pictures of the port. She contacted the local police, and when they arrived, she stayed to help. Unaware of the edge of the pier, Dees stepped off backward and fell into the water. Because of the weight of her equipment, Dees was unable to right herself, and she drowned. Dees was pulled out of the water, but attempts to revive her failed. Dees was thirty-four years old and is survived by two children.

Beverly Sue Clark

Beverly Sue Clark was born on May 21, 1967. Clark enlisted in the army following her graduation from high school in Armagh, Pennsylvania. She attended basic training at Fort Dix, New Jersey, and advanced individual training at Fort Lee, Virginia, as a material storage and handling specialist. Later, Clark went to the 2703 Reserve Forces School in Pittsburgh, where she was trained as a water purification specialist. Following an assignment with the 1,004th General Supply Company, Clark was then assigned to the Fourteenth Quartermaster Detachment, a water purification unit.

During Operation Desert Shield, the Fourteenth Quartermaster Detachment was one of twenty-two units from the Ninety-ninth Army Reserve Command to be activated. The unit underwent intense training, at Fort Lee, Virginia, in preparation for deployment to Saudi Arabia. For thirty days, Clark's detachment trained for eighteen hours a day on the reverse osmosis water purification unit (ROWPU), a water purification system. This system was used to produce clean water from undrinkable sources.

Clark's unit arrived in Dhahran, Saudi Arabia, on February 19, 1991. Just five days later, on February 25, 1991, Clark was killed during a Scud missile attack. A Scud missile hit Clark's barracks, a converted warehouse, while many of the soldiers were eating dinner, sleeping, and relaxing. In this Scud attack, twenty-eight soldiers lost their lives and ninety-nine others were wounded. In honor of Clark, an Indiana University of Pennsylvania scholarship was established for the children of the veterans of the Persian Gulf War. Clark received many decorations during her military career, including the National Defense Service Medal, the Southwest

Asia Service Medal, the Army Service Ribbon, and the Kuwait Liberation Medal. Clark was also awarded the Purple Heart for having sacrificed her life.

Christine Mayes

Christine Mayes was born in 1968 in Rochester Mills, Pennsylvania. After she graduated from high school in 1987, Mayes enlisted in the United States Army. She attended both basic and advanced individual training as a food service specialist at Fort Jackson, South Carolina. Of her three years of active duty, Mayes served two and a

Massive repairs took place after an Iraqi Scud missile hit a U.S. military barrack in Dhahran, Saudi Arabia, on February 25, 1991. Workers used cranes and other heavy machinery to quickly clean up the rubble.

THE PURPLE HEART

The Purple Heart was initially created in 1782 by the first president of the United States, George Washington, and was called the Badge of Military Merit. The award was a purple cloth heart and was designed to be worn over the left breast of the recipient's uniform. The Purple Heart, as it is known today, was reestablished in 1932 on the 200th anniversary of the birth of President Washington.

First Lieutenant Annie G. Fox

The Purple Heart, now a medallion, is awarded to members of the United States armed forces who are wounded by an instrument of war in the hands of an enemy. It is also awarded to the next of kin of those who are killed in action or who die later from wounds that they received in action. The first woman to receive a Purple Heart was Lieutenant Annie G. Fox, who was wounded during the Japanese attack on Pearl Harbor on December 7, 1941.

half years with the 586th Maintenance Company in Germany. In 1990, Mayes was released from active duty. She then enlisted in the army reserve, where she was assigned to the Fourteenth Quartermaster Detachment in Greensburg, Pennsylvania.

When Operation Desert Shield began in 1990, Mayes's unit was one of the twenty-two units activated from the Ninety-ninth U.S. Reserve Command, the parent unit of the Fourteenth. In the gulf, her unit served to purify, store, distribute, and issue drinkable water to the ground troops around her. Mayes performed her duty for five days before she was killed in action by the same

Scud missile attack that killed Beverly Sue Clark. The attack took place just hours before orders that told enemy troops to withdraw were announced over

This is the Purple Heart that is currently awarded by the United States military. While the original Purple Heart was made of cloth, the modern version is a medal bordered in gold that hangs from a purple and white ribbon.

WOMEN IN MILITARY SERVICE FOR AMERICA MEMORIAL

The Women in Military Service for America Memorial is a living memorial that honors all of the military women who have served, are serving, and will serve on behalf of the United States of America. It is located at the entrance to Arlington National Cemetery in Arlington, Virginia, just south of Washington, D.C. On November 6, 1986, President Ronald Reagan signed legislation authorizing the building of the women's memorial. A retired air force brigadier, Wilma Vaught, then spearheaded a campaign that raised more than $20 million to fund its construction. Ground was broken for the memorial in 1995, and it was finally dedicated on October 18, 1997.

Visitors to the memorial can view the fourteen exhibit areas that display the artifacts, photographs, and writings that were donated by servicewomen and their relatives. Quotes from military service-women, etched on a glass arch on the upper terrace of the memorial, represent a sort of journal compiled of women's voices. There are also film presentations, shown in a 196-seat theater, that portray the roles that women have played throughout America's military history. The Hall of Honor recognizes those women who have made extraordinary sacrifices, such as those who were taken prisoner of war and those who died in service. A computerized registry at the memorial is updated regularly and contains hundreds of thousands of personal biographies of some of the 2 million women who have served from the American Revolution to the present day.

Women in Military Service for America Memorial, in Washington, D.C.

Iraqi radio. Mayes, who had gotten engaged just one day before she left for the gulf, was twenty-two when she died. Mayes received the Army Reserve Component Achievement Medal, the National Defense Service Medal, the Southwest Asia Service Medal, the Army Service Ribbon, the Kuwait Liberation Medal (Saudi Arabia), and the Purple Heart.

Marie T. Rossi-Cayton

Major Marie Therese Rossi-Cayton, a native of Oradell, New Jersey, was born on January 3, 1959. Rossi-Cayton graduated from River Dell Regional High School and entered Dickinson College in Pennsylvania in the autumn of 1976. In 1980, she graduated with a psychology degree from Dickinson College, where she was an ROTC cadet. During the Persian Gulf War, Rossi-Cayton was the commanding officer of Company B, Second Battalion, 159th Aviation Regiment, and Eighteenth Aviation Brigade. She piloted a CH-47D Chinook cargo helicopter, in which she carried supplies to the troops in the combat zone. One-hundred sixty-three CH-47Ds took part in Operations Desert Shield and Desert Storm. In addition to their use in the transportation of troops, artillery, supplies, and equipment to the battlefield, these aircraft were also used for medical evacuation, parachute drops, search and rescue, heavy construction, and firefighting.

Rossi-Cayton's unit was among the first American units to cross into Iraq when the ground war of Operation Desert Storm began. Even though female helicopter pilots had taken part in

CH-47 Chinook helicopters airlift artillery pieces during a joint U.S. Air Force and Army exercise. Chinooks were crucial to Operation Desert Storm and Operation Enduring Freedom. Chinook helicopters have been used by the U.S. military since the Vietnam War.

In a military funeral, the body of Marie T. Rossi-Cayton is honored at Arlington National Cemetery on March 11, 1991. The epitaph on her grave commemorates her as the "First Female Combat Commander to Fly into Battle."

the 1989 invasion of Panama for Operation Just Cause, this marked the first time that they had crossed a front line. As the 82nd and 101st Airborne Divisions advanced into enemy-held territory, Rossi-Cayton's unit supplied them with needed fuel and ammunition. In an interview conducted by CNN the day before the ground phase of Operation Desert Storm began, Rossi-Cayton showed her willingness for battle when she stated, "this is the moment that anybody trains for, so I feel ready for the challenge."[1]

Rossi-Cayton died on the night of March 1, 1991, the day after the cease-fire had come into effect. She was killed in a helicopter crash near her base in northern Saudi Arabia as she was returning from a supply mission. Rossi-Cayton had been flying in bad weather when her helicopter hit an unlighted microwave tower. Along with Rossi-Cayton, three other members of her crew were killed in the crash. The U.S. Army honored her sacrifice in 1992 by naming a small-arms development and testing facility at the Picatinny Arsenal in Dover, New Jersey, the Marie T. Rossi-Cayton Building Armament Technology Facility. In that same year, she was inducted into the Army Aviation Hall of Fame. Rossi-Cayton, who was laid to rest in Arlington Cemetery, was the only female casualty of the Gulf War who was honored in that way. Her gravestone reads, "First Female Combat Commander to Fly into Battle."

Cindy M. Beaudoin

Cindy M. Beaudoin was born on July 20, 1971, in Putman, Connecticut. During the Persian Gulf War, Beaudoin served in the 142nd Medical

In 1782, George Washington designed this original Purple Heart badge and stated that it should be awarded to anyone who had done a "singularly meritorious action." Those who wore the Purple Heart were given special privileges such as the right to pass by guards without question.

Company of the National Guard as a medic. She was killed in action on February 28, 1991, just hours after a cease-fire was declared.

Beaudoin had been providing medical attention to surrendered enemy soldiers at the Iraq-Kuwait border when an explosion killed her platoon commander and wounded several other members of her platoon. She quickly readied herself to fight, but a second explosion mortally wounded her. In a letter that she had written for her parents to open in the event of her death, Beaudoin asked them not to mourn for her. She asked for them, instead, to mourn for all of the men and women who had given their lives so that others could live freely. For her sacrifice, Beaudoin was awarded the Purple Heart.

After the Storm

The years following the Persian Gulf War saw changes in the policies and laws governing the roles that women were allowed to play in the military. The women who participated in Operation Desert Shield and Operation Desert Storm did more than just help to liberate Kuwait. Their performances opened up many new roles and thus thousands of positions, to females in the military. Shortly after the war's end in 1991, Congress repealed the law that restricted women from flying in combat aircraft. This meant that air force and navy women would now be able to pilot fighter and bomber planes. Then, in 1993, the ban on women serving on combat ships was lifted. With the exception of submarines, navy women are now able to serve on all combat vessels. This includes destroyers, aircraft carriers, and frigates. Then in 1994, Congress set policies that allow women to take part in combat support near the battlefields.

In the recent conflict in the Middle East, women participated in far more roles and comprised an even larger percentage of the armed forces than they did during the Gulf War. Operation Iraqi Freedom, also called Persian Gulf II, began on March 20, 2003, after Saddam

Hussein failed to live up to the agreements of his 1991 surrender. In this war, army and marine women, who are allowed in ground combat, came closer to the front lines than ever before. Air force and navy women flew in combat aircraft, and women were aboard almost all navy vessels. Navy women, like Heather O'Donnell, Jenn Stillings, and Shannon Callahan, flew combat missions as electronic countermeasures officers, working to jam enemy radar and communications signals. As in the first Persian Gulf War, women were also killed and taken as prisoners of war. In one such case, on March 23, 2003, three female army soldiers were among a dozen who were ambushed when their convoy took a wrong turn in the desert. One of these women died, and the other two, who were taken prisoner, were later rescued.

Though women are now serving in virtually every area of the military, there are some positions that are still closed to them. Women are still not assigned to frontline combat and are not allowed to serve in units in which they would be likely to see ground combat, such as tank, infantry, and artillery units. As well, army women are not permitted to serve in special operations units, such as the U.S. Army Rangers. Air force women are still not allowed to be paratroopers, those trained to parachute from an aircraft, or combat controllers, personnel who are trained to take over runways so that military aircraft can land. Submarine warfare is still closed to navy women, as is the special operations unit of the Navy SEALs (sea, air, land). Though not allowed to serve in all military positions, women have been praised for their quality of work in the positions in which they do serve. This thought was captured by Rhonda Cornum, former Desert Storm POW, and is etched in a glass panel of the Women in Military Service for America Memorial in Arlington, Virginia: "The qualities that are most important in all military jobs—things like integrity, moral courage, and determination—have nothing to do with gender."

TIMELINE

August 2, 1990	Iraq invades Kuwait. President George H. W. Bush orders trade with Iraq to stop.
August 7, 1990	Operation Desert Shield begins as the first fighter planes arrive in Saudi Arabia.
August 22, 1990	President Bush calls up reservists to active duty.
November 22, 1990	President Bush visits U.S. troops for Thanksgiving Day.
November 29, 1990	The United Nations authorizes the use of force if Iraq does not leave Kuwait by January 15, 1991.
January 15, 1991	The deadline for Iraq to withdraw passes.
January 17, 1991	The air war phase of Operation Desert Storm begins.
February 23, 1991	Iraqis set fire to approximately 700 oil wells in Kuwait.
February 24, 1991	The ground phase of Operation Desert Storm begins, with army troops and marines moving into Iraq and Kuwait.
February 25, 1991	An Iraqi Scud missile destroys U.S. barracks in Dhahran, Saudi Arabia, killing twenty-eight soldiers.
February 27, 1991	President Bush orders a cease-fire.
March 3, 1991	The first allied prisoners of war are freed.

Glossary

aircraft carrier A large warship that carries aircraft.

amass To accumulate or collect.

artillery Large mounted firing weapons.

battle group A naval force composed of a varied number of warships, escorts, and supply vessels.

brigade A military unit made up of a large number of troops.

coalition A group formed for a common purpose and for mutual benefit.

commission A rank given to an officer in the military.

deploy To bring military forces into action or to strategically distribute military forces.

destroyer A small warship.

dictator A ruler who has total authority.

direct commission If a person holds a college degree when entering the military, he or she may be given a rank in the military without having to attend basic training.

electromagnetic energy Energy that moves in a wavelike motion.

embargo A government order forbidding the trading of goods.

ensign A commissioned officer of the lowest rank of the navy.

fleet A number of warships operating together under one command.

frigate A medium-size U.S. warship.

howitzer A cannon.

infantry The part of the army that is trained to fight on foot.

logistician A military person who deals with the replacement and the distribution of material and personnel.

mechanize To equip with armed motor vehicles.

meteorologist One who studies weather and weather conditions.

NROTC Navy Reserve Officers Training Corps.

protocol officer An officer who deals with the code of ceremony and etiquette that the military follows.

radar A device used to determine the position, size, and velocity of a distant object.

reconnaissance The exploration of an area that provides military information.

requisition To demand things in order to meet the needs of the military.

reservists Fighting forces kept inactive until needed.

retaliatory Acting to punish a person or group for something they have done.

ROTC Reserve Officers Training Corps.

Scud Russian-made short-range missile.

theater An area of military operations.

ultimatum A final demand.

United Nations (UN) An international organization that was formed in 1945 and includes most of the countries of the world. It was formed to promote peace, security, and economic development.

United Nations Security Council The UN Security Council is responsible for maintaining international peace and security. The five permanent members are China, France, Russia, Great Britain, and the United States.

For More Information

U.S. Army Women's Museum
2100 Adams Avenue
Building P-5219
Fort Lee, VA 23801-2100
(804) 734-4327
Web site: http://www.awm.lee.army.mil

**Women in Military Service for
   America Memorial**
Ceremonial Entrance
Arlington National Cemetery
Arlington, VA 22211
(800) 222-2294 or (703) 533-1155
Web site: http://www.womensmemorial.org

WEB SITES
Due to the changing nature of Internet links, the
Rosen Publishing Group, Inc., has developed an
online list of Web sites related to the subject of
this book. This site is updated regularly. Please use
this link to access the list:

http://www.rosenlinks.com/aww/guwa

For Further Reading

Becraft, Carolyn. *Women in the U.S. Armed Services: The War in the Persian Gulf.* Washington, DC: Women's Research and Education Institute, 1991.

Breuer, William B. *War and American Women: Heroism, Deeds, and Controversy.* Westport, CT: Praeger Publishers, 1997.

David, Peter. *Triumph in the Desert: A Commemorative Photo History of the Gulf War.* New York: Random House, 1991.

Moore, Molly. *A Woman at War: Storming Kuwait with the U.S. Marines.* New York: Scribner's, 1993.

Weinstein, Laurie, and Christie C. White. *Wives & Warriors: Women and the Military in the United States and Canada.* Westport, CT: Bergin & Garvey, 1997.

Bibliography

Cornum, Rhonda, and Peter Copeland. *She Went to War: The Rhonda Cornum Story.* Novato, CA: Presidio Press, 1992.

Farrel, John Aloysius. "Female Troops Are Getting Closer to Combat Than Ever in U.S. History." *Boston Globe,* January 28, 1991.

Goodman, Ellen. "Military Myths Meet Reality." *Boston Globe,* April 21, 1991.

Gugliotta, Guy. "A Woman's Place: In Command." *Washington Post,* January 23, 1991, pp. B1, B9.

Gugliotta, Guy. "Scuds Put U.S. Women on Front Line." *Washington Post,* January 28, 1991, pp. A1, A9.

Holm, Maj. Gen. Jeanne. *Women in the Military: An Unfinished Revolution,* revised edition. Novato, CA: Presidio Press, 1992.

Jewish Virtual Library Web site. "Lisa Stein." 2003. Retrieved May 2003 (http://www.usisrael.org/jsource/biography/lisastein.html).

Kaplan, Fred. "Women Push Limits on Combat Roles." *Boston Globe,* May 28, 1991.

Moses, Phyllis R. "Swinging on a Star." *Woman Pilot Magazine.* 1993–2002. Retrieved May 2003 (http://www.webcom.com/pilot/wpmag/past%20issue%

20pages/2000%20issues/mar%20april%202000/
swing.htm).

Nickerson, Colin. "Combat Barrier Blurs for
Women on the Front Line." *Boston Globe*,
November 13, 1990.

P.O.W Network Web site. "Bio, Rathbun-Nealy,
Melissa." March 9, 1991. Retrieved May 2003
(http://www.pownetwork.org/gulf/rd035.htm).

Powell, Stewart M. "More Voices from the War."
Air Force Magazine, June 1991, Vol. 74, No. 6.

Ralston, Jeannie. "Women's Work." *Life*, May
1991, p. 56.

Randolph, Laura B. "The Untold Story of Black
Women in the Gulf War." *Ebony*, September
1991, Vol. 26, No. 11, p. 100.

Riggs, AT1(AW). "Commanding Officer." April 2,
2003. Retrieved May 2003 (http://www02.clf.
navy.mil/hc2/Executive/commanding_
officer.htm).

Stambaugh, J. J. "New Face Joins Media 'Troops'."
Knowville News/Sentinel, March 28, 2003, p. A13.

Sullivan, Joseph F. "Army Pilot's Death Stuns Her
New Jersey Neighbors." *New York Times*, March
7, 1991, p. B1.

U.S. Navy Office of Information Web site. "United
States Navy Biography, Elizabeth M. Morris."
March 25, 2002. Retrieved May 2003 (http://www.
chinfo.navy.mil/navpalib/people/flags/
biographies/morrisem.html).

U.S. Navy Office of Information Web site. "United States Navy Biography, Annette Elise Brown." November 21, 2002. Retrieved May 2003 (http://www.chinfo.navy.mil/navpalib/ people/flags/biographies/brownae.html).

U.S. Navy Office of Information Web site. "United States Navy Biography, Bonnie Potter." September 5, 2002. Retrieved May 2003 (http://www.chinfo.navy.mil/navpalib/people/ flags/biographies/potterb.html).

Voisin, Ailene. "Women at Military Schools." *Atlanta Constitution*, October 15, 1995.

Source Notes

Introduction
1. Appendix R, "Role of Women in the Theater of Operations" in *Conduct of the Persian Gulf War: Final Report to Congress.* Vol. 2. Washington, DC: Department of Defense, 1992.
2. Ibid.

Chapter 1
1. Phyllis R. Moses, "Swinging on a Star," *Woman Pilot Magazine.* 1993–2002. Retrieved May 2003 (http://www.webcom.com/pilot/wpmag/past%20 issue%20pages/2000%20issues/mar%20april% 202000/swing.htm).
2. Maj. Gen. Jeanne Holm, *Women in the Military: An Unfinished Revolution* (Novato, CA: Presidio Press, 1992), p. 444.
3. Ibid.
4. Moses.
5. Jewish Virtual Library, "Lisa Stein." 2003. Retrieved May 2003 (http://www.us-israel.org/ jsource/biography/lisastein.html).
6. Muhammad Sadiq and John C. McCain, *The Gulf War Aftermath, an Environmental Tragedy* (Boston: Kluwer Academic Publishers, 1993), p. 2.
7. Guy Gugliotta, "Scuds Put U.S. Women on Front Lines," *Washington Post,* January 28, 1991, p. A1.
8. Ibid.

9. U.S. Air Force, "F-15 Eagle." Retrieved May 2003 (http://www.af.mil/news/factsheets/F_15_Eagle.html).
10. D'Ann Campbell, "Combatting the Gender Gap [Part 1 of 3]," *Contemporary Women's Issues Database* (Farmington Hills, MI: 1992), pp.13–23.
11. Peter Grier, "A Quarter Century of AWACS," *Air Force Magazine,* March 2002, Vol. 85, No. 3.
12. Stewart M. Powell, "More Voices From the War," *Air Force Magazine,* June 1991, Vol. 74, No. 6.
13. Holm, p. 452.

Chapter 2
1. Fred Kaplan, "Women Push Limits on Combat Roles," *Boston Globe,* May 28, 1991.
2. Ibid.
3. Ellen Goodman, "Military Myths Meet Reality," *Boston Globe,* April 21, 1991.
4. Laura B. Randolph, "The Untold Story of Black Women in the Gulf War," *Ebony,* September 1991, Vol. 26, No. 11, p. 100.
5. Ibid.
6. Ibid.
7. Ibid.

Chapter 3
1. Dee Finne, "Tailhook—Both Sides." 2001. Retrieved May 2003 (http://www02.clf.navy.mil/hc2/Executive/commanding_officer.htm).
2. Judith Bellafaire, "Contributions of Hispanic Servicewomen," *Women in Military Service for America Memorial,* 1997. Retrieved May 2003 (http://www.womensmemorial.org/HisHistory.html).

Chapter 4

1. Maj. Gen. Jeanne Holm, *Women in the Military: An Unfinished Revolution*, revised edition (Navato, CA: Presidio Press, 1992), p. 457.
2. Michelle Koidin, "Female POW: I Wasn't a Hero," The Associated Press, January 16, 2001.
3. Diane Jennings, "U.S. Women Endured Captivity in 1991 War," Knight-Ridder/Tribune News Service, March 24, 2003.
4. Greg Barrett, "Treatment Was Bad, but Got Better for Female POW in First Gulf War." Gannett News Service, March 26, 2003.
5. Rhonda Cornum, *She Went to War: The Rhonda Cornum Story* (Novato, CA: Presidio Press, 1992), p. 123.
6. Barrett.

Chapter 5

1. Science Applications International Corporation. "Rossi-Cayton." Retrieved May 2003 (http://www.quad-a.org/Hall_of_Fame/rossi-cayton.htm).

Index

About the Author

Heather Elizabeth Hasan graduated college summa cum laude with a dual major in biochemistry and chemistry. She currently resides in Montgomery County, Maryland, with her husband, Omar, and her son, Samuel.

Photo Credits

Front cover, pp. 10, 20, 40, 68 courtesy of Defense Visual Information Center; back cover, p. 94 U.S. Army Center of Military History; p. 5 © Reuters NewMedia, Inc./Corbis; p. 7 © Jacques Langevin/Corbis Sygma; p. 13 © Dennis Brack; p. 15 © David Turnley/Corbis; p. 17 © Bettmann/Corbis; p. 22 courtesy of Jewish Women's Archive (http://www.jwa.org); pp. 23, 30, 51, 57, 84–85 © AP/Wide World Photos; p. 25 © Peter Turnley/Corbis; pp. 26–27 © Hulton Archive/Getty Images; p. 34 © Cynthia Johnson/Time Life Pictures/Getty Images; p. 35 U.S. Army photo; p. 43 © Getty Images; p. 47 © Donna Ferrato; p. 55 © Steve Kaufman/Corbis; pp. 60–61 U.S. Navy photo; p. 63 Photographer's Mate 3rd Class Jayme Pastoric/U.S. Navy; p. 66 courtesy of Naval Historical Center; p. 74 © Richard Mason/*Army Times*; pp. 76–77 © George Hall/Corbis; p. 81 © Lee Snider/Corbis; p. 86 National Personnel Record Center, National Archives and Records Administration; p. 87 © Nathan Benn/Corbis; p. 89 © Orion Photography, courtesy of the Women's Memorial; p. 91 © Corbis; p. 92 © J. L. Atlan/Corbis Sygma.

Designer: Evelyn Horovicz;
Photo Researcher: Peter Tomlinson